MOTHERLOVER

Motherlover
© 2015 Ginger Ko
20 19 18 17 16   1 2 3 4 5
Second Edition

Design & composition: Shanna Compton, shannacompton.com
Cover art: Sofi Thanhauser, www.sofithanhauser.com, sofithanhauser@gmail.com

Published by Bloof Books
www.bloofbooks.com
New Jersey

Member of CLMP

Bloof Books are printed in the USA by Bookmobile and Spencer Printing. Booksellers, libraries, and other institutions may order direct from us by contacting sales@bloofbooks.com. POD copies are distributed via Ingram, Baker & Taylor, and other wholesalers. Individuals may purchase our books direct from our website, from online retailers such as Amazon.com, or request them from their favorite bookstores.

Please support your local independent bookseller whenever possible.

ISBN-13: 978-0-9965868-2-5
ISBN-10: 0-9965868-2-2

1. American poetry—21st century. 2. Poets, American—21st century.

∞ This paper meets the requirements of ANSI/NISO Z39.48-1992

MOTHERLOVER

GINGER KO

CONTENTS

7   GASLIGHT

BODY

23   Natural
24   The afternoon, and other places too
25   Easter Egg
26   Émigré
27   Stay Away from My Windows No One Is Welcome
29   Frenemy
30   Nine-Tailed Fox Is Reborn in the Wrong Country
32   Treespeak
33   Baby Shower
36   Crouching down to crawl beneath, letting the desk enfold me, I curl up for secular dreams. Where is my legacy? Not here.
37   Love List
38   Shift some sharp things around and your face becomes familiar
39   I'm Wide Awake in This Recurring Dream
40   Flora
41   Get the fuck out woodland creatures, get the fuck out low-hanging fruit
42   Iterations:
43   Starve the Beast
44   I don't beg for a place to land but I feel lonely when you're drunk
45   Prayer for What's Close

PRAIRIE LIGHTHOUSE

49   Night Signature
50   Day Mark
51   Night Signature

52	Night Signature
53	Day Mark
54	Night Signature
55	Night Signature
56	Night Signature
57	Night Signature
58	Day Mark
59	Day Mark
60	Day Mark
61	Day Mark
62	Day Mark
63	Day Mark
64	Night Signature
65	Night Signature
66	Night Signature
67	Night Signature
68	Day Mark
69	Day Mark
70	Day Mark
71	Night Signature
72	Day Mark
73	Night Signature
74	Day Mark
75	Night Signature
77	ACKNOWLEDGMENTS
78	ABOUT THE AUTHOR
79	PRAISE FOR MOTHERLOVER

GASLIGHT

She wanted more
How could she get more
Looking through eyes that see nothing but dark blue blood
Running a tongue over secret small teeth
Gray and crowded
Things unremembered can be made unreal
A soft black eye perfectly round
Flavory fucking that fills the room
With a sodden smell

Circling in a round cloth house
Trying to remain uninterested in a seat at the table
Folie à deux cracked open when the younger winced at an ear itch
Guts lined with wet fur that had never seen light

Suddenly a difference
Sent to illumine the insides

But you'd fly into rages anyway
So even when I speak softly
How about I make myself a ghost
How about I really do what you say I'm doing
And protest with silent jowls
So if we'd lived on the moon
Where shadows don't cross your face
As quickly as you believe
What would you have done
Would you have cut the gut
From the inadequate ribcage
What would you do to my resting bitch face
Bobbing unbelievable accuser
Bearing up to me with your rotten
Little morsels of bonkers

Most nights I think I feel the weight of you
    But in the morning your side of the bed is empty and ambiguous
I haven't seen you in weeks
    Either you still love me or haven't come back for your clothes

The tight powder of shame cakes her face
    Stirring the bedsheets into a paste
She knew what was good, knew she was good
Carefully, carefully, all that body
Nothing making sense
    Settling tiny paper airplanes into trees
        Empty veins lining their surfaces
    Paper blank and brilliantly white
      Flying off with wind
    To always be there
To always be wiping, to not care
        Leaking molten and building the landscape again and again
    Every day branches brightening

What if I just stopped
What if decomposition sweetened me up a little

You pried through my entire childhood
But a child isn't allowed to feel sorry for herself

If she first doesn't have sorriness for you

If I were muscular enough, cunning enough,
To write entire books, to sing entire albums, to cut entire films,

About how you are wrong, the story of it
Consumable again and again

Lined with gold razor-wire flowers to punish
Those taking what isn't theirs

When I was young you'd take me to the movies.
You'd be furious afterwards if there were sex scenes.
I've been sorry to you my whole life
that you couldn't prevent bad things from happening to me.

With a cough she had never been so afraid.
A cough through a hole
In the back of the closet.

He had been there long
And now casually cleared his throat
Of such a thingness.

You beat me because the bag
of self betrays you,
gives and slides around your pinky freshness.
When you slice me open,
cutting the bright perfect rind,
you see the insides green and black,
putrid little girl bangs swirled inside with other rot.
Perfect squares, average circles.

I sat on the ground while your friends sat at dinner.
In front of my little friends you complained
about the dirt on my neck.
I don't remember you
or your nodding pungent
late-night guests
ever telling me how to wash my neck.

She pointed out a hawk in a tree
ripping at something that looked like nothing
but strong bright blood.
She wanted to hear the sagging sacks
of music box melodies, wanted to gloat
and say "Do you see that there?
It means nothing to me, nothing."

I don't make sense of your magnificence
tipping it out to see the suffocated swarming of roots
in the shape of their container
trapping the heat—setting the soil on fire.
I need you to destroy me, to catch me and engulf me.

Instead: a metronome on the slowest setting
for a song that lasts the rest of your life.
Pour down powdered glass to break the bones
but even my darkest animal is bright pink
at the point of severance.

Again and again I bury you after
I find you cold in the morning.
Still I never regret your blowing float
each time the ugly mouth and beautiful hands
each time the pretty lips, harmful fingers.

Your hands already swinging away.
Your body already dropping away.
Your face is so far away.
A dear face.
Unclear face.

BODY

NATURAL

there will only ever be one
bird but I won't describe its colors just
    that it fluttered in a shallow
    dip in the dirt and was so
    young it fell in the gutter and was
    swallowed by one of the many
    streams of the sea
and what is this wolf
    one of which I've never seen
        without a broad grin of suffering
I hear no angels in the music of a difficult landscape
            hear instead the wind
feel leaves pat you on the head
hail has hatched the eggs early
a bit of ocean in a cup
a bit of sky in my lungs
    color doesn't reach me here

THE AFTERNOON, AND OTHER PLACES TOO

      Glows through the icy rims of your ears
And the tips of your milky fingers
      Which are delicately freckled like seafood

You pat your skin still so dewy plump and say
      Maybe I shouldn't even be here
You say this to me
Who has fought for years to get here
And the world lifts you by the armpits
      Gently dips you in
Then lifts you out again

Against a dirty nape with curdled creases
      I strive much in this little life
With such repeated wave-like flinging
      I muster the missing materials
Onto itchy sizzled shoulders
      They give a kind of ivory quality pleasure

EASTER EGG

I don't want to go back to old lives: always give me new.
Am I your sister or your lover: or your mother.
Hoist the rabbit by its tail: the smallest thing without pinching.
Small wooden cages: seeds turning inside.
I will always be your stranger: love me alone or leave me alone.
Lumpen silhouettes: small grazing in the grass.
Look at all these waxy buds: branches soon impenetrable.
The ground is softening: raising up the smell of offspring and ghosts.

ÉMIGRÉ

it's a festering ingot in my mouth   some have thought to have seen a golden throat but it is   a sloppily cooled metal bar   warty from bubbling   from being dropped onto a dried clay floor   most of her twentieth year was being pregnant   she heaved she said   when her sister drowned   she lay in bed and felt as though hands jerked   her shoulders from behind and the next morning   a face-down body they had to buy   canvas slippers to lay at the crematorium   and then a whole new world   automobiles   the world connected by pavement   so much singing instead of bawling   testiness instead of suicide   how far back do cemeteries go in this country   what is done with all the anticipated bodies   or do all just live forever   so what's the use of invocations and reverie   only sometimes it boils up and I hear   how they swallowed poisoned pigeon feed   how they bashed their heads against the mouth of a water well   how they hated   molten and slow-moving   this thick batter of fire   dripping from the lip of the bowl   into my mouth

STAY AWAY FROM MY WINDOWS
NO ONE IS WELCOME

For many years I met expectations:
Packed a tiny mound of rice and lay myself down on it

Stretched out to wait for someone's
One-bite-two-chew swallow

That type of someone always reminded me
That my boobs can be cupcakes

Lots of things I've done have felt like
Drinking the worst tequila from the tip

Of a dick-shaped shooter made of ice
So you always make it my responsibility

To explain what's happening to you
Do you think I'm some kind of torch singer

I'm on fire
You're on fire

No one ever listens when they ask
Except later when they crash into my words

And think they're listening to themselves
I'm a daughter and used to remaining unmentioned

As legacy at funerals
I'm a thirty-year-old woman

Accustomed to men who don't believe me
When the mail key sticks or when

Situations aren't pithy or when
Indoor dogs don't wake for rain

FRENEMY

Cool cool you've learned how to breathe freely cool for you
You boom your voice with such bravado that you choke a mosh pit
I actually enjoy your straight-backed chanting
With your mouth agape so different from my cross-legged keening
I want to be cool about thinking aloud how do I do that
How do I get enough lip to cover the molar rows on my palate
How do I sew the stomach that gapes fatty yellow
If I have no medical training
How kind sir do I learn to use your buckets of blood
Without trying to sop up the spray with a fur stole
How do I stop myself will you show how you shut me up and out
Oh like this with a _____ to my _____

NINE-TAILED FOX IS REBORN IN THE WRONG COUNTRY

Dear mother,
    pull the skirt tight against my thighs.

Dear car mechanic,
    break my right ankle to the side and stuff me with a seatbelt.

Dear hairdresser,
    suck until you choke on my straight black hair.

Dear father,
    break my nose with hardback books.

Dear little school friends,
    pluck long white overnight hairs from my forehead.

Dear school-bus driver,
    overpower my lap with your smooth heavy hips.

Dear ex-boyfriend,
    let me raise your ex-girlfriend's abortion for you.

Dear ex-husband,
    drive me to the ATM as if you had stopped for my bow-legged jangle.

Dear supervisor,
    bend me over by the bathroom potpourri.

Dear colleague,
    squeeze my tits together around the pen you dropped down my shirt.

Dear dentist,
    twist my shovel teeth around in their sockets so the little curves face out.

Dear stranger on the street,
    wedge your wet hot tongue under my eyelids.

TREESPEAK

Everything we think to do, we do.

I told you I brewed up a fire, I set the sidewalk boiling, and soon all the cement panels were askew.

I actually don't care for your flowers, they're not ribbons at all, and I don't like to think of a sea of privates agog around me.

Who says we feel more than the wind in our uppermost, we look through our roots, we crowd into dirt as hard as rock and uplift skeletons.

It's an imposition to bring myself to meet the springy bulges of your staring, your recognition.

So are you going to save me?

Let's not glorify the outdoors anymore, it wouldn't be so bad to live inside a well-windowed house.

I have felt so much with these crusts.

The shadows of your neighbors look much like your own: admit it.

BABY SHOWER

In front of my mother I dig all my fingertips into my chin, and it's true, I've wasted a lot of time. You wait until your body has given up, is what you do. She nods and chews her tongue knowingly, as if mealy with banana.

You have such a pretty little yard, little baby. I'll walk the perimeter and report to your parents any holes in the fence.

After I hit him in the face, he went to his father's dog-sitter to ask about the nature of enduring love. She an old alcoholic who used to be the most beautiful woman in Wyoming. Has accepted God and lives alone. What was her answer I wonder.

She was wearing a droopy bikini, vomiting into the toilet, when the cruise ship began throbbing. "Nooo!" she wailed. "Our baby was conceived in HELL."

✳

So much time in the shade, so much time alone. I dislike the grandeur of illness that is a kind of dying. My body bearing up under puzzlement. So many years preparing. For nothing, it turns out.

✳

When he closed the door behind him, I wept as bitterly as the time I watched fragile kittens stumble inside a small cage.

✳

Tears sloppy like raw egg whites with self-pity. Afterward the skin on my cheeks frescoed hard and glossy. It could be a tragic Greek mask but I'm actually OK.

✳

A bright day for a house party, the breeze bringing glittering gems to the branches. A cluster of balloons rising straight and fast while in the distance a dust devil lifts up an empty pizza box that flaps like a gull.

✳

If we ever get back together, I'll be brave enough to call him Babe.

*

The slide show ends, but the soundtrack was inexpertly timed and shuts off midsong. I clasp my hands beneath the plastic tablecloth.

CROUCHING DOWN TO CRAWL BENEATH, LETTING THE DESK ENFOLD ME, I CURL UP FOR SECULAR DREAMS. WHERE IS MY LEGACY? NOT HERE.

In dreams I am no one's lover. I wake up, find my fingers do not meet when handling your throat with both hands.

But I do so love the smell of your detergent, your muscled neck scent, the smell of your neck above a clean shirt.

There must be something terribly wrong: I find I can't live without most of your body, but would snip out nerves that roll your eyes upwards.

In fact, the whole neck-up situation: the throat that voices dum-dum things, the b-boying eyebrows, the dented forehead brim.

The lovely Eastwood tweaking of your cheek when you switch between kissing different corners of my mouth. When windy-kissing, how your beard is Velcro for my flying hair. Oh well!

I washed my hair today, I thought it was about time. Shampooed twice, stood wondering about the world outside the second-floor bathroom in a three-bedroom townhouse.

In life I belong to no one, not even a house cat. Who signs up for this? Perhaps many, with varying amounts of wisdom.

LOVE LIST

We talk to each other at home
    moving around   shouting everything twice
      into the dryer
      the fridge
      the empty dog crate
And nowadays
Your sleeping self feels
so entitled
    to space in the bed
    to air in the room
    to time with your twitches
    to configurations   with my patience
      in the curdy light of morning

SHIFT SOME SHARP THINGS AROUND AND YOUR FACE BECOMES FAMILIAR

So I let out some love
You like me better deflated

Some kind of bird is singing between our houses in the middle of night
That can catch its breath without ceasing its song

Twenty times I hear a cat land on the floor in the apartment upstairs
Becoming an inexplicable secret that makes you responsible to your
    family and friends

You don't give permission to enter, so the threshold tears my skin off
I revel in your angry horror and with no cheeks my teeth grin

My fucking floor, you shout, and all over again I feel foolish
My only family

When we tore each other up we could only come back halfway,
    prodigal with harm
So you look and I am always

Touch me and I am always
I can sit like a stone until the day you will be coming for I am always

I'M WIDE AWAKE IN THIS RECURRING DREAM

My fight through disappointment days long
Eats through all small happiness

With a fever that burns you
Down to the ribs and beaming skull

You can hardly wait for me to leave the house
So you can tighten your brace alone

And I can't stop punishing you
I could have you anytime

I can't stop watching myself from a distance
As my splitjaw gapes

Like a triumphant snake's

FLORA

You called to tell me "The money's good—I'm ready to be married!" but we had already wed years ago.

    I am disgusting. Raised to be a bride, to hate myself for it, I come to you full of brides.

        There is no room in my heart for important men who surround themselves with flowers. Take the garland of wives and daughters from around your neck. That you feel safe they would not choke you makes me sick.

        Floating flowers. As if you are the bowl in which water rises. Fucker.

I laughed "You're silly!" and then ran to the bathroom to give myself a bloody nose. Surging in pulses

        until a rope of saturated snot snakes from my sinuses. Thick cherry mud patted into gifts and then ossified by sun.

GET THE FUCK OUT WOODLAND CREATURES, GET THE FUCK OUT LOW-HANGING FRUIT

The back of my tongue has craved bitterness for days.
    I crack into raw potatoes, look for the cigarettes
there, but end up with umami.

I twist myself into lingering trash so your low
    summer waters miss me on the bank.
Help me find my birth family.

I put away the trophy won from pressing the bridge
    of my nose against your neck. For love I do it,
eking bruise-colored ghosts from a glass dropper, I do it.

And speaking never to myself but to you,
    to you, to you. Even in my head, to you.
And the unbearable reverence brought on

by selfhood sniped, dropping straighter
    than the strongest wind. Dive-recalled to earth—
unbearable teeth snap it out of the air.

Its teeth, its teeth, its skeleton-key teeth.
    And before: how we meandered, never quite
as true as when ridiculous.

You left for the mountain angrily—
    you realized you had to shovel the driveway first,
and then you left for the mountain angrily.

ITERATIONS:

A new boy, different dog, our small apartment.
I'm not sick, I swear.
I just keep believing:
I deserve this,
I should keep trying,
This is what I want,
I deserve this,
I should have it,
I'm not sick, I swear.

STARVE THE BEAST

When what you want doesn't matter to the one you love
You swam around inside   felt me rock with rubato
Feathers stuck beneath your eyelids   don't you dare rub them
Or you'll spark your dry mind   on fire
A giant snake wrapped around the cone of a volcano and when I stuck a straw
in the mouth earwig after earwig dripped out and thudded far below
I'll clutch this in me forever and make   an unalterable
Easy pain   hardscrabble pleasure   shower of scavenger shit
Muddled   muddled   troubled
You pathetic arrested thing   Heart!   Parcel out what ails you so that we
can start living well

I DON'T BEG FOR A PLACE TO LAND BUT I FEEL LONELY WHEN YOU'RE DRUNK

      When you fall asleep I try on your eyeglasses:
the top of my skull breaks off
      and floats with the gentle heat of a lamp.
Why don't you come over?
      Everything that's crushed into creasing,
you can have those things.
      I'm sorry, don't you worry, that you leave
the night soundly by making yourself heavy.
      I only pity you, that's the way it is,
that's the stiffness in your arms after you climb into bed
      and lock me against your chest,
that's your even breathing.
      Teeth so tight that the tongue is mangled,
and the crown of my head pivots like a parachute.

PRAYER FOR WHAT'S CLOSE

Let me stay here in the West please God
Let me live on in shabby comfort
Let me find the tinned tomatoes aisle without wandering
Let me feel safe enough to have children someday

I'll make every day worthy and won't be unpleasant
I'll remember not to dissolve into a malcontent
I'll breathe and other cleansing things
I'll wake in the mornings and write affirmations

> Such as If I bother eating vitamins then I should admit I'm interested
> Such as I'm lucky to have this guy and mustn't grind him down even if he lets me
> Such as I can be cool and lucky when I choose
> Such as (guy again because he's important) His mouth parted and flush

And with a pen's ink that's indelible my God
    I promise I'm not changeable just look at what I've been praying all these years
        Gripping snowflakes with pinches
I'm ready for the sharpness of this because now I know that it'll be sharp

This thing which is summer without mosquitoes and some sunshine
  why not
This thing which is a lovely life
This thing which is unpacking
This thing which is picking a spot on the wall for a picture as if it
  mattered dear God

PRAIRIE LIGHTHOUSE

NIGHT SIGNATURE

I don't feel all right,
plunging under.
Above all I'm rooted
to the edge of the sea.
Peek through the window,
see me eating my vitamins.

DAY MARK

The rest of her life she breathed in time to the beacon.
There was nothing on the island but a fortress and my mother.
When she married she left.

NIGHT SIGNATURE

It is a chalky little ovoid, a little boiled egg rolling out to the edge of a cliff as I hold it under my tongue during a gulp from a glass.

Little nongeneric bouncing around, agitated to pieces so it can travel to that place between my eyes that holds a tight kaboom.

This is the place, I'm told, that holds those terrible impulses, but I think something else: it is the bracelets of pulse at the ends of my arms, or the skin wrapping my thighs, or all these wicked little parts that now squeeze in the dark.

NIGHT SIGNATURE

everything beneath the snow is straw colored
    a silly color for despair

blowing and glowing, the color of creek is the color of light
    all this insincerity in love stuff

rather, everything is dully colored and rattles dry
    early summer trees still wearing pine cone crowns

I try so hard to be a neutral person
    when I'm not, people ask me why not

    the ghost of your cologne isn't romantic anymore

DAY MARK

"The break, the break" he kept exclaiming
 until I squinted and saw the tiny white muff of waves
 in the crotch of some hills: "Huh."

NIGHT SIGNATURE

"A fire tower," he soothed. "Or a dried-out peak of rock."
NO NO NO—look at this surrounding sea of churning shortgrass.
I dare you to deny I am a prairie lighthouse.

NIGHT SIGNATURE

Someone I have never met turns off all the lights of their house, the front of which I know as well as my collected dogs, freeway curves, and frozen-mud trails

My sternum aches with that hateful straightness used when we raise up our voices, grimacing with the mouths of ocean-floor fish

With desperation strong as anger I wish for a slight reversal of time; an ant field bustles continuously on my left cheek

NIGHT SIGNATURE

Your prehensile smile

and then
the silent suddenness of skunk smell!

NIGHT SIGNATURE

Nighttime always a soft orange, I sit up in it and look out your barred first-floor window. Wailing tomcats in heat stalk the front garden back and forth.

Last night we stood in the cold while a train rushed riverlike in the distance. We were so high up that tears left my eyes in plumes and floated all around us.

I haven't been alone in days, and now that I am I still speak to you. Why weird the grayscale quality of my life, I ask you.

DAY MARK

Don't toss the Coin Flip app
or shake the Magic 8 Ball
to see if I'm leaving you.
I'm right here. Here.

DAY MARK

Wash the baby, wash the baby, the little girl chants,
knocking dolly's forehead
against the washboard

DAY MARK

What is this pale tenderness
            that is like standing at the top inside a fog
I wait for the familiar temperature trickle

If it doesn't hurt
    is it still right
If it isn't fierce
    is it still strong

DAY MARK

Euphoria in winter, what dumbassery.
    (Stupid sneaky snakes of sidewalk ice can suck a dick.)
There is always a hollow cold, swiping the inside of a drinking cup
    with a dry hand.
    (Help. Stop. No, you stop what you're doing and help me start.)
Am I an old biddy who dusts teacups?
My house keeps sinking and the lawn is up to the windows.
Every morning I keep stirring up oatmeal.
    (Steel-cut foods keep me depressed all day.)
I feel like a beast but I am unsure I'll ever feel beastly again

DAY MARK

    We water the high plains,
        luxurious sprinkler fanning a curtain of water
back and forth on the lawn,
        as indolent as a showgirl's
            feathered fan.
Evenings we play cornhole on bright grass.
        Snap suspenders, belt out fusty falsettos.
        Oh here comes the hook
from the side of the stage.

DAY MARK

I wear wooden shoes
for you

NIGHT SIGNATURE

The water isn't quite hot enough to release the stain from the tea bag.

[something something sentimental]

My palms smell like I've been hanging on to metal.

The parts even grime can't reach my body fills with sick-smelling sebum.

With the jaggedness of underwater darting you open the kitchen window.

Let wind whisk the pancake mix.

NIGHT SIGNATURE

Things go sluggish, then things go normal.
I lie back on a creek and melted-snow waters weigh on my chest in a knife's shape.
    I float prone and try to forget I'm prone. My sinking feet keep
    kicking up silt clouds from the bed,
        and I do not wash very far downstream.

I am not afraid to fly with a chip on my shoulder.
    A snatch of smell or shake of sound will pull a lever in my heart
    and my body floods with wings.
The glowing hump of a rat moving aside ivy, the wasp thunking against plaster
    incite grievances in my pulse, but persuasion is of a preserving
    nature, and I can retreat towertop, alone
where anyone can see me and glare into the plains.

NIGHT SIGNATURE

You don't let me finish drowning.
"Doll face," you call, and my lips and eyes freeze midbreath.
Maskfaced, I watch you walk to me in the dark.
Lay me down, lay me down, so that my doll-lids can close.

NIGHT SIGNATURE

The panic of tangling my legs
in your underwater hair

The dread of touching the unlit earth
at the roots of high grass

DAY MARK

Animal grief: perfect remembrance of a night.
    Understanding in ways that build guilt—it's not a tragic innocence
        (your pet dog biding at the train station).

    And later,
  when my favorite snacks are perfect ripe seedless grapes
I peel with fingernails.
    Patience and loyalty very unlike love.

DAY MARK

Held so tightly I jumbled.
Under evening or dawn,
the rumbling of on-ramps,
the damp droning of HVACs,
I rode the train to baste
under bare bulbs.

So I ran away,
a crumple in the middle
of a giant's footprint. Ridiculous.
But maybe I am happy like this,
I am in the sun,
I spot lovers in town
but do not speak
to them later about it.
I have been dropped
to the ground at
the relaxing of a fist.

DAY MARK

I lost my dogs
I lost my Marlboros
I lost my neighbors
I picked up an e-cigarette at the local head shop
and the glowing blue tip lights up space in bed
(for I also lost my lamp)
I lost my thirst
I lost my faith
Blue blue beacon
I lost the charm

NIGHT SIGNATURE

I could never love you
who would never hurt me

DAY MARK

When I got what I wanted, I gave up the things that got me what I wanted,

says almost no one I've known

NIGHT SIGNATURE

My self-sufficiency has disappeared. I pick up five-dollar pulp books

    when I buy cigarettes and I read them at home
        in front of television talk shows.

I cannot quit racing through the empty calories.

    I choose the wordiest books, the angriest show panels,
        to dash words against my senselessness.

At night I must turn off lights, click the set, and lie in bed like a
    drowned flower,

    dried spice, a glass mannequin filling out my clothes.
        I feel around my head with taps of recognition.

I remember how it feels, but have forgotten how to get there.

    I point a flashlight at darkness,
        the light dissipating before touching on a single thing.

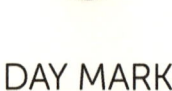

DAY MARK

May this range be one of work and love

NIGHT SIGNATURE

From the top of the fortress two leaps of light take turns

ACKNOWLEDGMENTS

My thanks to the following journals, in which variations of these poems first appeared:

Anti-, Bone Bouquet, Deluge, Hot Metal Bridge, inter|rupture, Likewise Folio, smoking glue gun, the *Pinch Literary Journal,* the *Quotidian Bee, Toad, TYPO,* and *Vector Press.*

My thanks to Danielle Pafunda, Andy Fitch, Jeff Lockwood, Beth Loffreda, Harvey Hix, and Kate Northrop for their kindness and guiding vibes—toward my work, and toward my person generally.

My thanks to Sofi Thanhauser for the beautiful book cover, and to Shanna Compton for giving the book beauty and care.

My thanks to my family: my parents, Pearl, Lam, and Jack.

My thanks to Shawn for being there when it all happens

ABOUT THE AUTHOR

Ginger Ko is from California. Her chapbooks *Inherit* (Bloof) and *Comorbid* (Lark Books) are forthcoming. *Motherlover* is her first book. She wrote it in Wyoming.

PRAISE FOR MOTHERLOVER

Ginger Ko's *Motherlover* is at once supplication and rebuff. I've been going back again and again to the book for its moments of airtight agony, unsparing in their demands. Despite everything: *Motherlover* doesn't want your sympathy. *Motherlover* doesn't want your disdain. *Motherlover* doesn't want your loyalty, even. It only wants you to let it alone, sit back down, and think about the errors of your ways.

—***Fanzine*, Grace Shuyi Liew**

The speaker, who is multivoiced yet tonally consistent, presents a daughter, a wife, and, at times, the vestige of a mother; she talks of and to a mother, a father, and a partner. This underlying question operates on a practical and psychological level: who am I to you? The closing section's title seems to grow out of the opening's: the "Gaslight," the small flickering streetlight that can reveal but a small part of blanketed darkness where *Motherlover* started, is now a "Prairie Lighthouse," a towering flare giving glimpses onto a three-hundred-and-sixty-degree world, which much like a prairie fades out at the distant horizon. As Ko's speaker concludes, "From the top of the fortress two leaps of light take turns." Two beams alternate, attempting to light up the darkness. This is not just a work of agony—it's a work seeking restoration out of a damaging pattern and into an illuminated horizon.

—***Entropy*, Tim Etzkorn**

www.ingramcontent.com/pod-product-compliance
Lightning Source LLC
Chambersburg PA
CBHW020958090426
42736CB00010B/1372